Prayers of Real Stories

Vicki Oberski

Copyright © Vicki Oberski 2024

All Rights Reserved

All rights reserved. No part of this publication may be reproduced, distributed, or transmitted in any form or by any means, including photocopying, recording, or other electronic or mechanical methods, without the author's prior written permission, except in the case of brief quotations embodied in critical reviews and certain other non-commercial uses permitted by copyright law. For permission requests, please get in touch with the author.

Contents

Dedications i
About the Author ii
Diana and Covid 1
Diana'a Hair 3
Bethann Prays 4
Leigha's Angel 5
Donna's Prayer 6
Boat Miracle 7
Floated on a Lake 8
Nick's Adventure 9
Saved by an Angel 10
Susan's Graduation 11
Vicki's Car Miracle 12
Lynn's Prayers 13
Marie Sunday's 14
Nick and Heaven 15
Valorie's Prayer 16
Pray 17
Norma's Prayer 18
Sandy's Test 19
Wendalyn's Keys 20
Teddy's Cure 21
Scripture Quotes 22
Sara 24

Dedications

I've dedicated this book to my family and friends, who have helped me to write the book, and whom I couldn't do without them. To the Lord as well, who helps every day.

About the Author

I've written this book to help people learn about real stories, answered prayers, and faith in their lives.

Answered prayers are good for anyone to hear it in their lives. I've had personal answers to prayers that have helped me and my family and boosted my faith.

I'm a quiet personality with a little dog, Teddy, a Pomeranian and family. I like books and to read and knit and crochet. I hope these stories help others in their lives to have answered prayers too.

Diana and Covid

Diana, my Mom had Covid, so did Vicki, and my sister Candy had it; we all did. Diana went to the hospital first. She had a temperature of 104° and fainted in the kitchen.

We were concerned and thought to pick her up on the floor, but then called an ambulance. They whisked her away, and in the emergency room, she was given a clot-busting drug. She then bled into her lungs as she reacted to the drugs. She coughed blood all over her, and she died for 8 minutes.

The doctors and the nurses fought to save her life. Meanwhile, Diana heard them say code blue! She's coded.

She saw all the people working on her. Then Mom slipped into a peaceful realm, one of beautiful, calming peace. She said she thinks the soul goes on and felt God was with her.

Mom reflects on her experience and tells her story to others, and they like it and ask questions. She's feeling better and living life to the fullest in the best way.

Diana'a Hair

Diana, Mom had sparse hair from having Covid. It was sparse, very thin in spots. She felt shy about going out to see family and friends or going to stores. Also, she stayed home a lot for weeks.

We, all her family, prayed for her every day, for her hair to come back. Online, it said people lost hair after having Covid, and it should come back in 3 months or 6 months! That's a long time to wait for your hair.

Well, after prayer, lots, Diana prayed too, and we all noticed 3-5 new hairs at first. Then in came more the next week, and in came her hair bit by bit until she actually tried a new perm. She has a little bit more to go, having 3/4 back after one month.

She'll probably have fuller hair completely in less time than we thought. We plan to pray for a cousin next; she doesn't know it, but we'll try to see who needs help next! Prayers work.

Bethann Prays

Bethann wasn't a winter person, as the snow was all over her car during these months. It frosted her windshield and was hard to scrape and brush off her car.

Her driveway was difficult to clear away with snow blowing. Hence, roads become unsafe to travel, with snow blowing spinning around and with low visibility. One can fall on ice hidden under the snow, she thought.

So, as she was going on a walk one day, cold and snowy, Bethann decided to pray about it. She prayed that snow could be only 2 inches all winter long, El Nino-like, with hope and faith.

That winter, there were 2-3 inches a couple of times, all winter in her hometown. Just one time was such a blessing answer for her to be happy about.

Leigha's Angel

Leigha was driving a van along the road, going home. She had prayed to see an angel, and wow!

One did appear in the back of the van window. The angel was as pretty as one could be; the angel's face was beautiful and prettier than a human could be!

Then Leigha looked away for a second or two and looked back to see her again. But she disappeared, not there. Leigha surely had an answer to a prayer. She was in wonder about her miracle.

Never did she think she'd have a heavenly angel so beautiful it would take your breath away. Leighas couldn't believe she'd seen her angel, but she was thankful and wished she could see another angel some day and would like to hug her.

Donna's Prayer

Donna was a young lady, 20 years old, and she wanted a job as a bookkeeper. So, she prayed to God she would give him a car and a TV set to her Mother in exchange for a job.

Donna waited, and sure enough, her phone rang, and yes, her job called her for an interview. While working then, Donna kept her promise and bought her Mother a car and a TV set. She was happy to have that new job. Prayers and a promise.

Donna loved her new job typing and bookkeeping, which kept her busy and happy. She drove and borrowed her mom's new car from time to time. She's very glad she prayed and had a super answer too. Her Mother drove her new car and watched TV, a winning answer for everyone.

Boat Miracle

My sister, Sissy, and me, Jenny, were with Dad in Uncle Beaver's boat at the Lake. As we floated along in the boat, Sissy said they pulled and pulled the boat motor, but it won't start!

Let's pray about this matter to God and see what might happen, we hope. They folded their hands, 5 and 6 years old, and prayed in earnest.

Then the boat started up instantly; pow! We giggled and were happy as could be with the kids answered prayers. The boat sailed on, and no one knew any better.

A fun boat ride was had by all, and two giggling girls were in the back seat. They felt so important that day, praying for the boat motor. The prayers of a child really matter. They grew up, still praying in their lives always.

Floated on a Lake

The three of us, Vivien, Lindsey, and Betty, floated out on a Lake on an air mattress, paddling away. We tried to go out by an island. It had seagulls on it and sandy shores, beaches, rocks, and trees in the breeze.

We three had fun on it, laughing and walking around kicking sand and completely alone. We worried a little bit and prayed we'd make it back safely paddle back to the regular beach shore.

Pretty soon, the coastguard showed up to come get us. The Coast Guard said someone called them about us; they thought we had fallen off a boat and needed rescue.

So, we giggled about it but felt goofy we attempted such a long ride on an air mattress. And we prayed to get home and wondered if the others who called prayed for us safely home, too.

Nick's Adventure

Nick was 62 years old and had dementia. He decided to go for a walk and always came back except once. He headed down a railroad track and walked 14 miles to the next town in Ossineke, Michigan.

Then Nick turned off in a yard and honked a car's horn for somebody to come out. A man came out of his house, and Nick said, "Do you have any mosquito dope?" (spray).

The nice man said, "I have better than that - I'll take you home. So they traveled in his car back to Nick's house. Nick's daughters and wife came out to thank the man.

He said: "Just call me his guardian angel." He had heard about Nick on his scanner. Prayers were said and answered.

Saved by an Angel

When Vicki was little, age 5, and out floating on an air mattress in Long Lake, Michigan, her Mom was by the shore watching her, floating out too far by some boats.

She paddled and tried paddling but was not able to get very far. She bowed her little head and hands folded, saying an urgent prayer. Her mom panicked; she couldn't swim very far.

Then, out of the blue, came a man dressed in all white. "Can I get her for you, Ma'am!" "Oh yes!" said Vicki's Mom. The nice man in white swam out to get Vicki and said, "Why didn't you paddle more to land? "She said, "I didn't know how."

The man in white pulled little Vicki out to shore. Mom was so happy her daughter was safe. Then her Mom turned to thank the man, but he was nowhere to be found. It must have been an angel!

Susan's Graduation

Susan was in a graduating ceremony at her senior high school, sitting in chairs with my class. Susan suddenly felt sickly cramps, stomach ache, and headache, so she squirmed in her green cap and gown.

Susan prayed nicely to Jesus and asked to be healed through the graduation and make it all the way through the ceremony. She made it through her big day and walked all the way home.

When Susan went to her house, she felt sick again and lay in bed. She said thank you, Lord. I felt good at graduation, and that was great. To herself, she thought, "I should've asked to make it through the whole day!" Not to be asking too much, though.

Susan was planning to feel good all day at graduation. She almost went home early to rest and feel better in time, missing her graduation. But praying sounded good and a little miracle helped the important day to go well.

Vicki's Car Miracle

When Vicki was stuck out of her car outside of a store, looking at plants, she locked her door and left her keys inside. She could see them through the window. The dog was inside with the keys, purse, and cell phone.

Vicki glanced at the window and noticed it was down a bit. She thought maybe she could reach her hand in to reach the button that unlocks the door. Oops, that didn't help.

Then, she tried the handle inside, and her car honked, honked, honked! The car must have been programmed to prevent someone from stealing the car. The car door popped open instantly.

Vicki knew the Lord had unlocked the car, she believed. She had to put the key in the door, and turn it to lock, then unlock it to stop the car alarm from going off. Vicki drove off happy she didn't need a tow truck and was safely home.

Lynn's Prayers

Lynn prays for traffic to lighten when she goes out driving her car. When there wasn't a chance to get out of traffic, she prayed for clearance.

And it would clear up a big space for her to leave on more than one occasion. It would be clear. Her grandma used to say, "You'll get your turn."

Lynn remembers those words to feel better to get a chance to get out on the road. Lynn even noticed clear roads out and about without prayers and just followed her around. Prayer sure helps to clear a good path.

Lynn likes her answers of clearing roads, and she thinks she's lucky. She continues to pray about it on the roads. Lynn keeps a stuffed angel and cross in her car to ensure safety in her travels.

The clear roads are always there in the early mornings, usually always. Her prayers are said and help with safety on the roads and in driving, and that's great.

Marie Sunday's

Marie was going to her job when she thought, oh no! I have to work on Sunday. What should I do about that? I'd rather be in church.

So she prayed she could have Sunday off and went to work. So then Marie asked her boss for Sunday off.

The boss said I'll do better and give you all Sunday's off! Just as nice as that.

Marie then went to church with a smile and was thankful for her nice answer to prayer. She likes her boss too.

Marie appreciated her Sundays were off from her job. She knew she had answers to her prayers. She meets people at her job and thinks it's a really nice place to work. She prays for others there as well. It pays to work with good folks.

Nick and Heaven

Nick had dementia and Alzheimer's and was in a nursing home for 2 years. His family prayed for him to get better all the time. They visited Nick a lot and prayed over him and for him all the time.

Nick's daughter asked him, Do you believe in God still? To reassure herself he'd remember. He said yes. About 2 years later, Dad died.

His daughter Vicki got the call and sighed sadly and then gazed out the window and saw 2 white angel wings tip out her window.

She was so reassured then that it was my Dad and it was about him - that we knew he was in heaven indeed.

Nick could remember his family barely and with a smile. He didn't get better or heal completely. But now in heaven we believe he remembers us, and at real peace. We never stopped praying for him and to get better.

Valorie's Prayer

Valorie was exercising with an exercise tape, which lasted about a half hour. Feeling all pretty good, she went about doing housework. When suddenly, her back went out, and she felt awful pain in her back; it hurts, she thought.

She couldn't move around too much, and the pain was there. Her father-in-law came over and took one look at Valorie, bent way over in pain, and said, "I got to go," scared of the way she looked.

She was all bent over and couldn't straighten up! Looking like an older woman. Valorie decided to call her Mom and sister and ask them to pray for her back.

Well then, within a half hour, Valorie sneezed and crackle, crack, snap! Her back went back to good shape. Feeling whole again, she called her Mom and sister and said thank you and, of course, said thank you to God for her miracle.

Pray

When you see the news on weather, and hurricanes are happening, or you need rainfall in your area, pray about it. Pray for hurricanes to slow down so it doesn't hurt land or people.

Hurricanes can slow from 130 mph to about 80 mph. Rain can be prayed about; farmers sure do, and have it rain in a couple of days. So when it rains, think of a farmer.

A person can pray about anything: flowers growing, pets' health, wars, family's health, weather, friends' health, and, of course, about yourself. Prayers matter in our lives. Pray, pray.

The prayers of a righteous man availeth much. James 5:16 We like answers, that's why we pray; you think sometimes you didn't get an answer, then a week or month later it happened your answer. Some answers happen right away; some are later. It is a good thing to pray to the Lord.

Norma's Prayer

When she was a young lady in a theater show, she enjoyed her movie experience with popcorn and a drink. The minute she itched her eye, out popped the contact lens.

"Wow, help me guys", she said to her friends, "I've lost my contact lens". Norma, of course, prayed about it and searched and searched for the missing lens.

Scared if she could find it, three of her friends looked and looked. It finally was underneath her seat, in the dark. Surely, an angel helped her find it.

This was answered prayers and a dirty contact lens to wash and wear again. Thankful.

Norma liked wearing contact lenses and did so for quite a few years. As time went on, she wore her contacts less and decided to opt for glasses. You can't lose those, she thought, or can you? She felt prayers were said with her that day and appreciated her contact lens found.

Sandy's Test

Sandy, when little and 8 years old in the 4th grade, she prayed because she had to take a test that was hard for her. Her friend Bethy got good grades from the teacher on her tests and always got an A.

Sandy was jealous of the favoritism from the teacher. So she prayed for her test to get an A also, then she'd be a favorite student too. Sandy turned in her paper, and she worked real hard on it; then the teacher called her over.

"Little Sandy, you just got a perfect score! Sandy was so excited she knew she had a prayer answered that day, and liked her friend and teacher again.

Sandy liked her class, and teacher, even her friend Bethy. She felt she had to get a good grade on her test to match up with Bethy. The prayers of a child really work - children's prayers are important. In the next grade and years, Sandy always used her prayers again.

Wendalyn's Keys

Wendalyn was out with her friend when she remembered she locked her keys in the house. Her friend said, "Oh no, my phone, tablet, knitting bag and cup of coffee are in your house too ". Wendalyn said, " I'm sorry".

Maybe when we get back from the farmers market, "I'll pick my lock with a paper clip or your key". Wendalyn prayed, and her friend did, too. Who wants to be outside when it's cold out.

Wendalyn tried once, twice, and four times, and then the door opened. It was prayers definitely that let them in the house that day! They were glad ladies to be inside safely.

Wendalyn visited the farmers market in town that day, and she hoped we'd be home unloading groceries that afternoon. We tried the landlord, who lives 35 miles away and tried family, but no one was home. Well, it turned out Wendalyn was a locksmith at heart; prayers were answered. Next, we put a key hidden to change her outcome.

Teddy's Cure

Teddy Bear is a spunky, little, happy 6 lb dog. He enjoys walking outside, barking at cars that go by, and at people walking their dogs. Teddy is 11 years old and has a few missing teeth.

One day, Teddy woke his family up 3 to 4 times, going out at night, even at 12 am or 2 am. Then he quit eating for 3 days. His family worried about him and prayed for him to feel better.

Teddy's Mom flea combed him and found a flea nest on his back where he couldn't reach there to scratch it. So, we washed him and combed the flea nest out. We prayed for him to eat again, too.

All of a sudden, Teddy started eating and sleeping in better. The fleas gone had made a difference. Praying for him really helped.

Teddy sure likes his walks outside, and he plays by throwing the toy over and over. So glad he's such a playful pal at 11 years old. He hopefully makes it to a longer life and sleeps well throughout the whole night. Just got to get him to like his teeth brushed!

Scripture Quotes

Pray without ceasing. 1 Thessalonians 5:17

Therefore, I tell you whatever you ask for in prayer believe you have received it, and it will be yours. Mark 11: 24

Likewise, the Spirit helps us with our weaknesses. For we do not know what to pray for as we ought, but the Spirit himself intercedes for us with groanings too deep for words. Romans 8:26

Continue steadfastly in prayer, being watchful in it, with thanksgiving. Colossians 4:2

The Lord is near to all who call on him, to all who call on him in truth. Psalm 145: 18

For thou art my hope, Lord, thou art my trust from my youth. Psalm 71:5 Be of good courage, and he shall strengthen your heart all ye that hope in the Lord. Psalm 31:24

For God so loved the world, that he gave his only begotten son, that whoever believes in him should not perish but have everlasting life. John 3:16

The word is a lamp unto my feet and a light unto my path. Psalm 119:105

What a glorious Lord God, who daily bears our burdens, also gives us our salvation. Psalm 68:19

Sing out his praises, bless his name, daily tell someone that God saves. Psalm 96:2

The Lord God is trustworthy in all he promises and faithful in all he does. Psalm 145:13

Sara

Sara was driving along the road, picked up her friend Sue, and delivering the city newspaper to her Aunt Phyllis. Sara told her friend, Sue, another friend, said dont drive this around, and this needs a ball joint replaced.

Sara worried about it but trusted the Ford Edge would drive well. As they tootled around, Sara said, I hope this doesn't konk out ever, and as they turned the corner, the Ford broke right into Aunt Phyllis's driveway. The wheel was caved in, bent sideways and couldn't move another inch.

Sara called for a tow truck to come, with Sara's cousin Penny talking and helping. Sara's insurance covered the tow truck and towed it to the mechanic's shop. We all prayed, and Sara said we're lucky this only happened on this side street and at Aunt's house.

We were helped by a cousin and were so glad for the Ford to break down at a family's house. Sara's vehicle worked for 2 more years, and then she bought a newer van and said whew, I'll get my car fixed sooner next time.

The Ford Edge lasted quite a few years for Sara. She sold it to a friend. Then, she bought a newer Chrysler van with heated seats. That's a blessing and a heated steering wheel. Sara says she will listen to mechanics better when to Not drive her car. Thankful again for her Ford konking out on a side little road, not a highway.

www.ingramcontent.com/pod-product-compliance
Lightning Source LLC
Chambersburg PA
CBHW050156130526
44590CB00044B/3370